Down & Dirty
The Secrets of Soil

Dirt or Soil
What's the Difference?

by Ellen Lawrence

Consultant:

Shawn W. Wallace
Department of Earth and Planetary Sciences
American Museum of Natural History
New York, New York

BEARPORT
PUBLISHING

New York, New York

Credits
Cover, © Alexander Raths/Shutterstock and © A. Linscott/Alamy; 4, © wawritto/Shutterstock; 5, © Jeff Thrower/Shutterstock; 6, © Pukhov Konstantin/Shutterstock; 7, © David Lade/Shutterstock; 7R, © sauletas/Shutterstock; 8, © Romolo Tavani/Shutterstock; 9, © Bogdan Wankowicz/Shutterstock; 10T, © kavalenkau/Shutterstock; 10B, © Chris Bernard Photography Inc./iStock; 11, © luckypic/Shutterstock; 12T, © Shutterstock; 12B, © Candus Camera/Shutterstock; 13, © Stephen Parker/Alamy; 14T, © age fotostock/Alamy; 14B, © Anton Foitin/Shutterstock; 15, © Holmes Garden Photos/Alamy; 16, © Eye of Science/Science Photo Library; 17, © Kokhanchikov/Shutterstock; 18, © Lev Kropotov/Shutterstock; 19, © Bill Brooks/Alamy; 20T, © mihalec/Shutterstock; 20B, © Shutterstock; 21, © Diana Mower/Shutterstock; 22, © Yala/Shutterstock, © Shutterstock, © Straight 8 Photography/Shutterstock, and © WilleeCole Photography/Shutterstock; 23TL, © balounm/Shutterstock; 23TC, © Eye of Science/Science Photo Library; 23TR, © Shutterstock; 23BL, © FotograFF/Shutterstock; 23BC, © Briana Hunter/Shutterstock; 23BR, © Dennis van de Water/Shutterstock.

Publisher: Kenn Goin
Editor: Jessica Rudolph
Creative Director: Spencer Brinker
Design: Emma Randall
Photo Researcher: Ruby Tuesday Books Ltd

Library of Congress Cataloging-in-Publication Data

Lawrence, Ellen, 1967– author.
  Dirt or soil : what's the difference? / by Ellen Lawrence.
      pages cm. — (Down & dirty : the secrets of soil)
  Summary: "In this book, readers learn what the difference is between dirt and soil."—
Provided by publisher.
  Audience: Ages 4–8.
  Includes bibliographical references and index.
  ISBN 978-1-62724-833-4 (library binding) — ISBN 1-62724-833-1 (library binding)
  1. Soil science—Juvenile literature. 2. Soils—Juvenile literature. 3. Soils—Classification—
Juvenile literature. I. Title.
  S591.3.L376 2016
  631.4—dc23
                              2015015249

For more information, write to Bearport Publishing Company, Inc., 45 West 21st Street, Suite 3B, New York, New York 10010. Printed in the United States of America.

10 9 8 7 6 5 4 3 2 1

Contents

Soil, Mud, and Dirt

When people play soccer, they often play on a grassy field.

The grass grows in moist, brown soil.

After a game, the players' clothes might be muddy from the soil.

Their shoes may be covered in dirt and will need to be cleaned.

Soil, mud, dirt—what's the difference? Let's investigate.

The soil beneath one soccer field can have about one million worms in it!

dirt

grassy soccer field

soil

In what ways do you think soil, mud, and dirt are similar? In what ways are they different?

5

What's Soil Made Of?

We see soil in gardens, parks, and on sports fields.

There is also soil beneath buildings, roads, and sidewalks.

So what is soil?

The main **ingredient** in soil is tiny grains of rock.

Soil also contains bits of dead plants.

When leaves fall from trees or flowers die, they rot and become part of the soil.

soil at a construction site

apples, leaves, and twigs rotting on the ground

a dead bird on the ground

When insects, birds, and other animals die, their bodies lie on the ground and rot. Then tiny pieces of bones, fur, feathers, and other body parts become part of the soil, too.

Plants Need Soil

Without soil, most plants could not survive.

Soil contains **nutrients** that plants need to stay healthy.

In order to grow, plants also need water.

When it rains, water collects in soil.

Plants use parts called roots to take in water and nutrients from soil.

grass

soil

roots

When a seed falls from a plant, it lies in the soil. Soon, a tiny new plant starts to grow. It gets water and nutrients from the soil—just like a fully grown plant.

new plant

seed

roots

9

What's Dirt?

Sometimes, people call the stuff that plants grow in by another name—dirt.

Its proper name, however, is soil. So what's dirt?

It's something that's messy, unwanted, and needs to be cleaned up.

Dirt is the grit and tiny pieces of trash on a sidewalk, and the dust on an unwashed car.

Pet hair and crumbs on a rug are dirt, too.

dirt on a car

dirt on a dog

If you have ever helped out in a garden, you might have gotten soil on your hands. The soil makes your hands dirty. When this happens, you can call the soil on your hands "dirt" because it's unwanted and must be washed off.

soil

dirt

A Place for Plants

There's another very important difference between soil and dirt.

Plants grow in soil but they can't grow in dirt.

If you tried to grow plants in the dirt that was swept up from a floor, they couldn't survive.

That's because dirt does not contain the water and nutrients that plants need.

a tree being planted in soil

dirt from a floor

Mud is soil that is mixed with lots of water. Mud can actually be soil or dirt. Why? Lots of wet, sticky mud in a garden or field can be a good place for plants to grow, so it's considered soil. Wet, sticky mud on your shoes, however, will make a mess in your home, so then it's dirt.

Different Types of Soil

Soil can be black or red, soft or hard, or moist or dry.

There are lots of different kinds of soil all over the world.

In a **rain forest**, the soil is soft and black.

It contains lots of water and nutrients to help many types of plants grow.

In a desert, cactuses grow in dry, stony soil with little water.

a giant rafflesia flower growing in rain forest soil

cactuses growing in desert soil

The tiny grains of rock that make up soil often give it its color. In the county of Devon, in England, the soil is red because it contains bits of red sandstone rock.

Scientists often say that soil is alive. What do you think this means?

red soil

Living Soil

Scientists say that soil is alive because it is home to plants and many other living things.

Ants, beetles, millipedes, worms, and other animals live in soil.

Tiny living things called **microbes** also live in soil.

Microbes are so small they can only be seen with a **microscope**.

They help to break down dead plants and animals and make them rot, which adds nutrients to the soil.

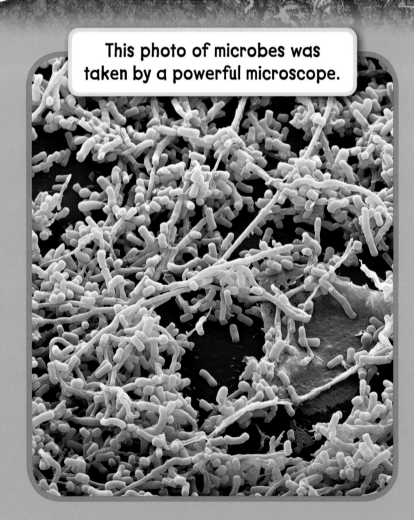

This photo of microbes was taken by a powerful microscope.

worms

As they wriggle around underground, worms feed on dead plants. Then their poop, which has lots of nutrients, becomes part of the soil.

Soil for Homes

Soil isn't only important to tiny animals.

Larger animals such as badgers and groundhogs dig burrows in soil.

These underground homes are safe places for animals to raise babies and hide from enemies.

People also need soil.

They build houses and apartments on it.

a house being built

soil

How do you think soil helps people get food?

18

Some animals need soil to survive cold winters. To keep warm, groundhogs spend winter resting underground. They stay in their burrows until the weather warms up in spring.

a groundhog peeking out from its burrow

We All Need Soil

People and animals don't need dirt, but they do need soil.

Without soil, animals wouldn't have plants to feed on.

Farmers would have nowhere to grow fruits and vegetables that people eat.

So sweep, vacuum, and wash dirt away, but be thankful for soil.

It gives us many things we need to live!

a goat eating grass

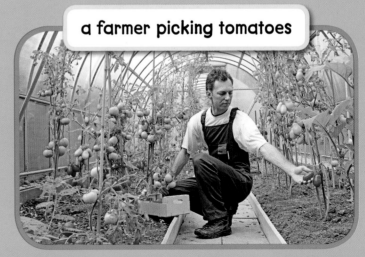

a farmer picking tomatoes

20

Trees and other plants make **oxygen** inside their leaves. People and animals need oxygen to breathe.

21

Science Lab

Let's Investigate Dirt and Soil

Go on a hunt to find soil and dirt in your home and neighborhood.

In a notebook, make a chart like the one on this page.

Describe the substances you find, and record whether they are soil or dirt.

You can begin by looking at the pictures below and answering the questions.

Which of these pictures show soil? Why? Which pictures show dirt? Why?

(The answers are on page 24.)

Soil	Dirt
Brown soil in planting pot in kitchen	Muddy footprint on porch
Stony soil in backyard garden	Dust on driveway

A   B   C   D

Science Words

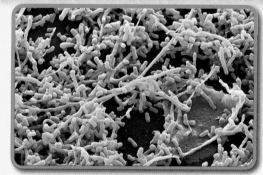

ingredient (in-GREE-dee-int) one of the materials that something is made from; rotting leaves are an ingredient in soil

microbes (MYE-krohbz) extremely tiny living things that can only be seen with a microscope

microscope (MYE-kruh-skohp) a tool used to see things that are too small to see with the eyes alone

nutrients (NOO-tree-ihnts) vitamins, minerals, and other substances needed by living things for health and growth

oxygen (OK-suh-juhn) a colorless gas found in air and water that people and animals need to breathe

rain forest (RAYN FOR-ist) a warm place where many trees grow and lots of rain falls

Index

Read More

Higgins, Nadia. *Experiment with a Plant's Living Environment (Lightning Bolt Books)*. Minneapolis, MN: Lerner (2015).

Lawrence, Ellen. *Dirt (FUN-damental Experiments)*. New York: Bearport (2013).

Troupe, Thomas Kingsley. *Diggin' Dirt: Science Adventures with Kitanai the Origami Dog*. North Mankato, MN: Picture Window Books (2013).

Learn More Online

To learn more about soil and dirt, visit
www.bearportpublishing.com/Down&Dirty

About the Author

Ellen Lawrence lives in the United Kingdom. Her favorite books to write are those about animals and nature. In fact, the first book Ellen bought for herself, when she was six years old, was the story of a gorilla named Patty Cake that was born in New York's Central Park Zoo.

Answers for Page 22

Pictures A and C are soil. Both the soil in the black tray and the farm soil have plants growing in them. Pictures B and D are dirt. These pictures show unwanted dirt and mud that must be cleaned up.